# A Pack of

# Wolves

Heinemann Library
Chicago, Illinois

**Richard and Louise Spilsbury**

Customer Service  888-454-2279

Visit our website at www.heinemannlibrary.com

Designed by Ron Kamen and Celia Floyd
Originated by Dot Gradations Ltd
Printed in Hong Kong, China by Wing King Tong

07 06 05 04 03
10 9 8 7 6 5 4 3 2 1

**Library of Congress Cataloging-in-Publication Data**

Spilsbury, Louise.
  A pack of wolves / Louise and Richard Spilsbury.
      p. cm. --  (Animal groups)
Summary: Describes the physical characteristics, behavior, habitat, and life cycle of wolves.
  ISBN 1-4034-0744-4 (HC),    1-4034-3285-6 (PB)
 1.  Wolves--Juvenile literature. [1. Wolves.] I. Spilsbury, Richard, 1963- II. Title.
  QL737.C22 S668 2003
  599.773--dc21

                          2002004036

**Acknowledgments**

The author and publishers are grateful to the following for permission to reproduce copyright material: pp. 4, 11, 17, 18 Gerard Lacz/FLPA; p. 5 Mark Newman/FLPA; p. 6 Uwe Walz/Bruce Coleman Collection; pp. 7, 12, 20 T. Kitchin and V. Hurst/NHPA; p. 9 Nigel Bean/Nature Picture Library; p. 10 Terry Whittaker/FLPA; pp. 13, 16 Daniel Cox/Oxford Scientific Films; pp. 14, 15, 19 Minden Pictures/FLPA; p. 21 Monty Sloan, www.wolfpaper/pl/photos; p. 22 Lon E. Lauber/Oxford Scientific Films; p. 23 Staffan Widstrand/Bruce Coleman Collection; pp. 24, 25 Corbis; p. 26 Marty Stouffer Prods/AA/Oxford Scientific Films; p. 28 Bruce Coleman Collection.

Cover photograph of an European gray wolf, reproduced with permission of Gerard Lacz/NHPA.

Some words are shown in bold, **like this.** You can find out what they mean by looking in the glossary.

# Contents

What Are Wolves?.....................................4

What Is a Wolf Pack Like? .................................6

Where Do Wolves Live? ...............................8

What Is a Territory? .................................9

What Do Wolves Eat? .................................11

How Do Wolves Hunt Together? .................................13

How Do Wolves Care for Their Young?.....................15

Do Wolves Talk to Each Other? .................................20

Do Wolf Packs Change? .................................23

Do Wolf Packs Fight? .................................24

What Dangers Do Wolves Face? .................................26

Wolf Facts.................................29

Glossary.................................30

More Books to Read.................................31

Index .................................32

# What Are Wolves?

Wolves are large, wild dogs. They have long legs, big feet, and a long, bushy tail. Most have a coat of thick hair. Adult male wolves are 5 to 6.5 feet (1.5 to 2 meters) long from the tip of the nose to the end of the tail. That length range is about the same as the height range for adult humans. Male wolves are about 30 inches (75 centimeters) tall. Females are a little smaller.

## Species of wolf

There are two **species** of wolf, the gray wolf and the red wolf. Gray wolves are larger. Surprisingly, gray wolves are not always gray. Most are gray to grayish brown. Some have reddish fur on the neck or patches of a different color. Others may be completely black, cream, or even white. Red wolves have shorter, redder hair. Both red and gray wolves are **endangered species.** Most do not live in the wild anymore but in special areas protected by people.

Most of the world's wolves are gray wolves, like this one. They look like German shepherd dogs, but they are more powerful. For example, their jaws are twice as strong!

4

# What Are Canines?

Wolves are members of the **canine** family. This includes species such as foxes, jackals, coyotes, and the dogs we keep as pets.

There are very few red wolves like these left in the world. Most live in parts of the southeastern United States.

## Groups of wolves

Wolves are **social** animals. Although each wolf does some things alone, it spends most of its time doing things in a group with other wolves. A group of wolves is called a pack. In this book, we will look at how packs of gray wolves live together in the wild.

# What Is a Wolf Pack Like?

A wolf pack is a family group. Most packs contain two parents and their young. Some packs also include a brother or sister of one of the parent wolves. Every wolf has a certain **rank**, or place, in the pack. Wolves know who is above them and who is below them in rank.

## Who's who in the pack?

The two parent wolves are called the **alpha** pair. They are the **dominant**, or top-ranking, wolves in the pack. The other wolves show respect to them and do what they want. The alpha male and alpha female usually decide what the pack does, such as choosing where to sleep and when to hunt. However, they do not tell the others what to do all the time.

**Most packs have about seven members, but people have seen packs of up to 36 wolves!**

The next most important members of a pack are the **beta** wolves. These wolves are usually between one and three years old. The older beta wolves are higher up than the younger beta wolves. The baby wolves, or **pups**, have their own ranking order that develops as they play.

## Knowing Your Place

You can usually tell which is the dominant wolf when any two wolves meet. The dominant wolf stands up tall with its tail up. Its ears point forward and it looks directly at the other wolf. The lower-ranking wolf crouches down, tucks its tail between its legs, holds its ears flat, and looks away from the dominant wolf.

A dominant wolf and a lower-ranking wolf show their rank almost every time they meet.

# Where Do Wolves Live?

Wolves can live in a lot of different places. They need what any other animal needs from a **habitat.** They need a supply of food, water to drink, and a safe place to raise their young. Wolves prefer areas with some place for them to rest or hide in, such as bushes or trees. They also avoid people as much as they can. They tend to live in wilderness areas such as hills, forests, or prairies.

## Around the world

Long ago, wolves lived all over the northern half of the world. Today, gray wolves live mainly in wild parts of North America, Asia, the Middle East, and a few parts of Europe.

**This white wolf is a kind of gray wolf that lives on Arctic tundra, land that is covered with ice and snow much of the year. Its white hair camouflages it in the snow.**

# What Is a Territory?

Each pack of wolves usually stays in a certain area, called its **territory**. This is the area in which they hunt, rest, sleep, play, and raise **pups**. A pack tries to stop wolves from other packs from going into its territory. Some packs have large territories. Others have smaller territories. The size of a territory depends on the amount of food that is available in it.

## Spring and summer territories

In spring and summer, a pack's territory is smaller than it is during winter. During spring and summer, there is a lot of food. There are more **prey** and their young around. Young prey are easier to catch. This is also the time when wolves have their young, and the adults never travel far from where the pups are kept.

In northern North America, a type of large deer called caribou spend the summer on the tundra. They travel hundreds of miles south to forests in winter. The wolves that eat the caribou follow them all the way.

## Fall and winter territories

In winter, food is harder to find. Some **prey** animals **migrate**, and others **hibernate**. Some are killed by the cold. The young prey are older and faster now, so they are not as easy to catch. The pack has to travel much farther to find prey and usually does not come back to the same spot each day.

## Scent marking territories

Just as people build walls or fences to stop others from walking on their property, wolves warn other packs to stay out of their **territory**. They mark an area by spraying a small amount of **urine** on objects, such as trees, rocks, or bushes. These **scent marks** warn other wolf packs to stay away.

Wolves can tell whether a scent mark was made by a wolf from their own pack or by a stranger.

10

# What Do Wolves Eat?

Wolves are **carnivores**, which means they eat the meat of animals. Wolves mainly eat large animals, such as deer, moose, caribou, and bison. These large animals provide them with lots of food. Wolves also eat smaller prey such as beavers, rabbits, squirrels, and fish. When they cannot find live prey, wolves will eat **carrion**— dead animals that have been killed by other animals, have died after being hurt, or have died from old age.

The only way wolves can catch animals that are larger and stronger than themselves is to hunt in groups. The wolves work together to catch the prey. This is one of the main reasons that wolves live in packs.

A wolf has 42 teeth. The longer fangs in front are sharp and curved for gripping prey tightly. Wolves use their other teeth to bite through flesh and bone and to grind their food.

# A Wolf's Leftovers

If the pack catches several large animals within a few days, they may not be able to eat all the meat at one time. Instead, they bury leftovers in an underground storage area, so they can eat the rest later.

## How much do wolves eat?

Once the wolves have caught an animal, they start to eat. Wolves usually go on eating until there is nothing left of the **prey** except the hooves and the biggest bones. Adult wolves can eat as much as 31 pounds (14 kilograms) at once. But they are not being greedy. It may be days before the pack catches another meal, so they have to eat as much as they can, when they can.

These wolves have killed a whitetail deer. They will hide the leftover meat to eat later.

# How Do Wolves Hunt Together?

Wolves usually hunt with their pack. When hunting, a wolf pack works as a team. Members of the team have different jobs to do. The **alpha** wolf usually tells them what to do and when to do it. When they go on a hunt, the wolves travel in single file. When they find prey, they usually **stalk** it first. They move silently until they are close enough to break into a run and attack.

## Finding Prey

Wolves find prey by coming across it by chance, smelling it from a distance, or following **scent trails**. Wolves have an excellent sense of smell. They can smell prey that is over a mile (1.6 kilometers) away!

Wolves hunt mostly at night, although they may hunt during the day in cold winters.

## Fast on Their Feet

Wolves usually jog along at about 5 miles (8 kilometers) per hour, but when chasing prey, they can run up to 45 miles (70 kilometers) per hour.

## Ways of hunting

Wolves have various ways of hunting. One or two wolves may chase a **prey** animal toward the rest of the pack. Sometimes the pack splits into two teams. The first chases the prey for a while, then the second takes over. This means they can keep chasing the prey until it is worn out.

A pack may chase a herd eight or nine times before they catch anything. Some scientists think they do this to find out which is the weakest and easiest animal to catch. When they have figured it out, they move in for the kill.

These Arctic wolves are chasing a herd of musk oxen. They will go after the weakest animal.

**14**

# How Do Wolves Care for Their Young?

The **alpha** pair in a pack usually stays together for life. Each year they **mate** and have a new **litter** of **pups**.

The alpha male and female mate in late winter to early spring, depending on where the pack lives. The new wolf pups are born about two months later. There are usually four to six pups in a litter.

## Wolf Pups

All wolf pups are born with dark fur and blue eyes. As they grow, their eyes turn yellow, gold, or orange.

The color of their fur changes, too. Even Arctic wolves, which have white fur as adults, are born with dark fur.

Wolf **pups** are born in a **den**, which is usually a hole underground. Wolves also use caves and hollow logs as dens. A den is usually near a river or lake so the mother does not have to go far from her pups to get water.

## The first weeks

The pups are born helpless, and their eyes and ears do not open until they are two weeks old. They begin to **suckle** from their mother right away. She stays in the den, which is often deep in the ground, caring for the pups until they are three or four weeks old and can walk.

While the mother wolf is in the den with the pups, the other wolves hunt and bring food for her to eat.

## When do pups leave the den?

The pups first leave the den when they are about a month old. The other wolves in the pack gather around to meet the pups as they come out. They all lick each other and wag their tails in excitement.

The whole pack helps care for the pups when they are out of the den. They all do their best to protect the pups. Each wolf watches out for eagles, bears, and other **predators** that would attack a pup.

When playing, the pups nip the ears and tails of the adults, and jump and climb on them. The adults are very patient. But if the pups get too rough, the adults let them know by showing their teeth.

## Who feeds the pups?

Soon the **pups** are ready to move on from their mother's milk to some meat. They are not old enough to hunt yet, so the other wolves bring food to them. The adults eat a lot of meat after a successful hunt. When they return, they feed the pups. To tell an adult that he or she is hungry, a pup licks the wolf's mouth. The adult spits up some chewed meat for the pup to eat.

## Play Time

Pups play together like many young animals do. They chase their own tails or jump at twigs or stones. They also play with each other a lot—wrestling, chasing, and pretend-fighting. Playing together helps them practice skills they will need when they are older, such as how to judge distances and how to react quickly.

When pups play, they figure out a **rank** order among themselves, which changes often. This helps them understand how the rank system in the pack works.

## A meeting place

When the pups are about two months old, the pack moves them from the **den** to an open area. This becomes the pack's new meeting place. The pups stay there all the time. The adults return there after hunting.

## Learning from others

When the pups are about three months old, they start to go along on some hunts. They watch the adults to learn what to do, what to catch, and how to follow **scent trails.** By winter, the young wolves are ready to travel and hunt with the rest of the pack.

When the adults in a wolf pack go out hunting, a low-ranking adult stays behind to baby-sit the pups.

19

# Do Wolves Talk to Each Other?

Wolves do not talk like we do, but they **communicate** in other ways. They make many sounds, including whimpers, growls, barks, whines, and pants, all of which mean different things. A growl means a wolf is not happy, and a whimper says that it is scared or hurt. Adult wolves hardly ever bark, but **pups** bark when they are playing or to call for help.

## Howling

A wolf's most famous sound is the howl. A wolf usually howls alone to find the rest of its pack or to attract a **mate**. When wolves howl together, they may be telling other wolf packs to keep away, helping the pack feel like a team before going on a hunt, or just howling for the fun of it!

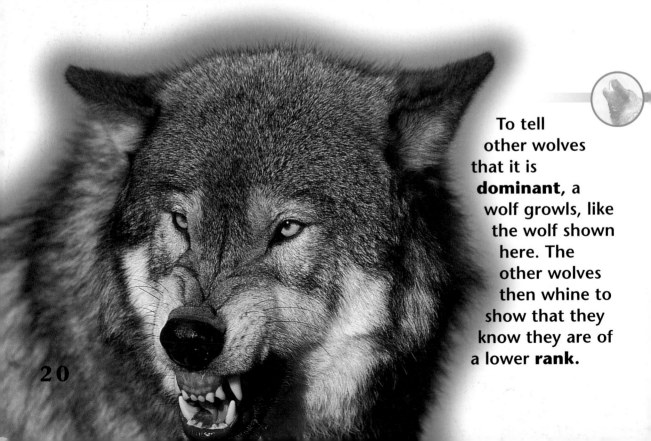

To tell other wolves that it is **dominant**, a wolf growls, like the wolf shown here. The other wolves then whine to show that they know they are of a lower **rank**.

Pictures of wolves
often show them
howling at the moon.
In fact, wolves may
howl at any time of
the day or night. When
a wolf pack howls all
together, other wolves
can hear it up to ten
miles (sixteen
kilometers) away.

21

## Body language

Wolves also use body parts to say other things and to signal their **rank** in the pack. A **pup** asks to play by bowing down with its rear in the air, tail wagging. If a wolf is angry with another wolf, it points its ears forward toward the other wolf.

## Communicating by smell

When wolves mark their **territories** with **urine**, they are using scent to **communicate**. When a wolf smells a **scent mark** like this, it can tell whether the wolf that left it is part of its own pack or not, how old it is, and even whether it is male or female!

**To greet an alpha wolf, a lower-ranking one nips at the center of the alpha wolf's muzzle.**

# Do Wolf Packs Change?

Wolf packs are constantly changing. Sometimes a pack forces out a sick, hurt, or old wolf that cannot hunt. They often let it follow behind and eat their leftovers. A young adult wolf usually leaves its parents' pack when it is about two years old. It may join with another single wolf to search for a new territory. They **mate** and have young and become the **alpha** pair of a new pack.

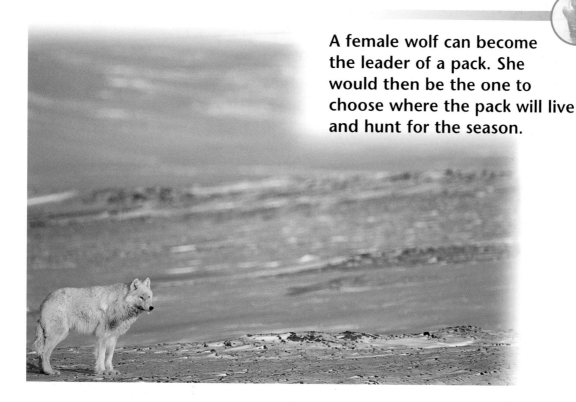

A female wolf can become the leader of a pack. She would then be the one to choose where the pack will live and hunt for the season.

## New alpha wolves

If an alpha wolf dies or gets too old to lead the pack, the remaining alpha may find a new partner from outside the pack. In some cases, the most important **beta** wolf takes over. He or she then chooses an outside wolf for a partner. Then they become the alpha pair of the pack.

23

# Do Wolf Packs Fight?

There is very little fighting within a wolf pack because each wolf knows its place, and the **rank** order helps keep the peace. Fights can happen when a pack is very large or when there is not enough food for everyone. Fights can end with a pack splitting into two or with one wolf leaving the pack.

Instead of fighting, a **dominant** wolf may crouch over a lower-ranking wolf, staring at it, showing its teeth, and growling. This warning is usually enough to stop any trouble.

## Fights with other packs

Just as wolves try to avoid fights within their packs, they also avoid fighting other wolf packs. The **scent marks** that wolves use to mark their pack's **territory** warn other wolves to keep away. This allows both packs to avoid a fight. Sometimes, though, when not much food is available, wolves wander into each other's territories in search of a meal. This may cause a fight.

# Peacekeeping

Wolves can usually avoid fights by using body language. A dominant wolf may remind a lesser wolf that it has more power by staring hard at it or nipping its **muzzle**. A lower-ranking wolf shows it does not want to fight by crouching down and flattening its ears.

The pack that claims the territory chases strangers away. If they do not leave fast enough, the two packs can end up fighting. Fights between different wolf packs often end with some wolves from each side being hurt or killed.

Wolves have strong bodies and sharp, powerful teeth for catching **prey.** They can cause serious damage to each other when they fight.

Wolves do not have many animal enemies. This is one advantage to living in a group. It is much more dangerous for another animal to attack a wolf that is part of a pack than it would be to attack a wolf on its own. The only wild animals that really threaten wolves are pumas and bears. These animals do not hunt adult wolves to eat them, but may hurt or kill wolves in fights over dead animals that one or the other has killed.

## Pup Problems

About half of the wolf **pups** born each year die before their first birthday. Many die from disease, fights, or accidents. Grizzly bears sometimes dig up **dens** to eat wolf pups while their mothers are away.

Wolves fight bears that try to take their food or get near their den. These fights can be rough, and wolves are often killed.

## A hard life

They may not have many **predators**, but wolves do not usually live more than ten years. They may be killed by disease, injuries, or **parasites.** Wolves may be hurt, or even killed, by large **prey** that defend themselves when wolves attack them.

## Wolves and people

A wolf pack's main enemy is people. Today, wolves are an **endangered species** because people have hunted and killed so many of them. Some people kill wolves for their fur or because they are afraid wolves might attack them. People also kill wolves because they are a danger to farm animals such as cattle and sheep. However, wolves only catch farm animals when they cannot find enough wild prey.

A moose can kill an attacking wolf by kicking out with its heavy hooves or using its sharp antlers.

## Territory troubles

People also harm wolf packs when they change the land that they live and hunt in. For example, when people cut down trees for wood or to clear land for farming or building, the deer that used to eat the forest plants starve. Wolf packs living there lose their homes and their food—the deer—so they eventually die as well.

## Protecting wolves

In many countries, laws stop people from hunting wolves or limit the number they can kill. People who know about wolves are teaching others that there is no need to fear these animals because they avoid people. In some places, such as **national parks**, taking steps like these has led to an increase in the number of wolves living there.

**In North America, wolves have not killed a single person for over 100 years. People, on the other hand, have killed thousands of wolves in that time.**

# Wolf Facts

## Where do wolves live?

Most of the world's gray wolves live in the map areas that are green.

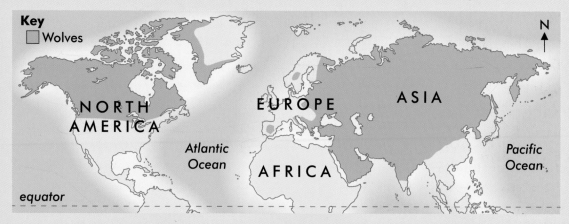

## Fast and silent

Wolves run on their toes, holding the back parts of their feet off the ground. This allows them to move very quickly and quietly. They can keep up a fast chase for about twenty minutes. Adult male wolves are 5 to 6.5 feet (1.5 to 2 meters) long, and they can leap up to 16.5 feet (5 meters) at a time.

## Wolves and prey populations

Wolves usually catch the weakest, oldest, or sickest animals in a herd. These animals are least likely to hurt the wolves and they are the easiest to catch. The weakest animals in a herd of deer are likely to die anyway, but in the meantime, they compete for food with the others. By killing them, wolves actually help to keep a herd healthy.

## Wolf sayings

In the past, people often were afraid of wolves. Many old sayings that mention wolves use them to mean something bad or evil. "A wolf in sheep's clothing" describes someone who is pretending to be good but is really bad.

# Glossary

**alpha**   used to describe the leading male or female wolf in a pack

**beta**   used to describe wolves that are below the alphas but above their brothers and sisters in the rank order

**camouflage**   colors and patterns that help an animal's body blend in with its background

**canine**   belonging to the dog family

**carrion**   meat from an animal that is already dead

**carnivore**   animal that mostly eats other animals

**communicate**   pass on information to another animal

**den**   place where baby wolves are born and where they live until they are about two months old

**dominant**   refers to the leader or most important member of a group

**endangered species**   any type of animal or plant that is in danger of dying out

**habitat**   place where an animal or plant lives in the wild

**hibernate**   go into a long and very deep sleep during cold weather

**litter**   young animals born at the same time to the same mother

**mate**   joining of a male and female of the same species to create young

**migrate**   when animals move from one place to another that is far away

**muzzle**   nose and mouth of an animal from the dog family

**national park**   area that is protected by law, so that people cannot harm the plants and animals that live there

**parasite**   animal or plant that lives on or inside another living thing

**predator**   animal that hunts other animals for food

**prey**   animal that is hunted and eaten by another animal

**pup**   wolf that is one year old or younger

**rank**   place in an order of things

**scent mark**   strong-smelling urine an animal has sprayed somewhere as a signal to other animals

**scent trail**   smell that an animal leaves behind on the ground that other animals can follow

**social**   living in well-organized groups that work together

**species**   group of living things that are alike in many ways and can mate to produce young

**stalk**   quietly sneak up on an animal in order to get close enough to catch it

**suckle**   when a baby animal drinks its mother's milk

**territory**   particular area that an animal or group of animals claims as its own

**urine**   liquid waste produced by an animal's body

# More Books to Read

Barrett, Jalma. *Wolf*. San Diego: Blackbirch Press, 2000.

Berger, Melvin and Gilda. *Why Do Wolves Howl?* New York: Scholastic, 2002.

Dudley, Karen. *Wolves*. Austin, Tex.: Raintree, 1998.

George, Michael. *Wolves*. Chanhassen, Minn.: Child's World, 1999.

Greenaway, Theresa. *Wolves, Wild Dogs, and Foxes*. Austin, Tex.: Raintree, 2001.

Martin, Patricia A. Fink. *Gray Wolves*. New York: Scholastic, 2002.

Myers, Jack. *How Dogs Came from Wolves*. Honesdale, Pa.: Boyds Mill Press, 2001.

Perry, Phyllis J. *Crafty Canines: Coyotes, Foxes, and Wolves*. New York: Franklin Watts, 2000.

Reid, Mary E. *Wolves and Other Wild Dogs, Vol. 10*. Chicago: World Book, 2002.

# Index

alpha wolves   6, 13, 15, 22, 23
Arctic wolf   8, 14, 15

bears   26
beta wolves   7, 23
body language   22, 25

camouflage   8
caribou   9
carnivores   11
carrion   11
communication   20–22

dangers   17, 26–28
dens   16, 26
dog family   5
dominant wolves   6, 7, 20, 22,
   24, 25

endangered species   4, 27

female wolves   4, 6, 15, 16, 23
fighting   24–25, 26
food   9, 10, 11–12, 16, 18, 24
food storage   12

gray wolf   4, 8, 29

habitat   8
howling   20, 21
hunting   11, 13–14, 19

male wolves   4, 6, 15

mating   15
meeting place   19

national parks   28

old and sick wolves   23

packs   5, 6, 9, 10, 11, 12, 13, 14, 15,
   17, 18, 19, 20, 21, 22, 23, 24–25, 26,
   28
play   17, 18
predators   17, 27
prey   9, 10, 11, 12, 13, 14, 27, 29
protecting wolves   28
pups   7, 9, 15–19, 20, 22, 26

ranking order   6, 7, 18, 20, 22, 24, 25
red wolf   4, 5

scent marks   10, 22, 24
scent trails   13, 19
size   4, 29
species of wolf   4
speed   14, 29
stalking   13
strength   4
suckling   16

teeth   11, 25
territory   9–10, 22, 23, 24, 25

wolf sayings   29